INFLUENCE AND

How to Win People Ove

Fiona Elsa Dent

60 Minutes Success Skills Series

First published 2000 by
David Grant Publishing Limited
80 Ridgeway
Pembury
Kent TN2 4EZ
United Kingdom
Tel/fax ++44 (0)1892 822886

03   02   01   00   10 9 8 7 6 5 4 3 2 1

60 Minutes Success Skills Series is an imprint of
David Grant Publishing Limited

British Library Cataloguing in Publication Data
A CIP catalogue record for this book is available from the British Library

ISBN 1-901306-32-1

Cover design: Liz Rowe
Text design: Graham Rich
Production coordinator: Paul Stringer
Edited and Typeset in Futura by Kate Williams
Printed and bound in Great Britain by
T.J. International Ltd, Padstow, Cornwall

This book is printed on acid-free paper

*The publishers accept no responsibility for any investment or financial decisions
made on the basis of the information in this book. Readers are advised always to
consult a qualified financial adviser.*

*All names mentioned in the text have been changed to protect the identity of the
business people involved. Any resemblance to existing companies or people is
entirely coincidental.*

CONTENTS

ABOUT *INFLUENCE AND SUCCEED!*

Can you learn about and get to grips with influencing in just one hour? The answer is a resounding "Yes!"

The ability to influence people positively is a vital skill for anyone working in today's busy, ever-changing business environment. This book aims to help you understand what influencing involves and to learn about the skills, approaches and techniques that are essential for influencing people successfully.

Is this book for you?

Influence and Succeed! is for people who find that in some instances they can influence others successfully but also find that in many instances they hit unanticipated barriers and are frustrated by their lack of success. Why is this? Why are some people easy to influence and others more difficult? This book is for you if you:

- ○ succeed but don't know why
- ○ sometimes fail to influence others
- ○ want to improve and extend your skills
- ○ want to adopt the right approach for different situations
- ○ are constantly compromising your ideas and plans
- ○ want to understand how to "influence without authority"
- ○ want to sell your ideas to others.

You will find out how to:

- ○ analyse the situation to ensure an effective outcome
- ○ plan and prepare effectively
- ○ decide upon the right tactics and approach for each situation
- ○ use your skills to best effect
- ○ get others to listen to you.

This book will help you to understand how you can be more successful when influencing others. It is not a theoretical tome or an exploration of the psychological concepts that affect influencing. It is designed to help you to understand the influencing process and to get better at it.

About the 60 Minutes series

The 60 Minutes Success Skills Series is for people with neither the time nor patience to trawl through acres of jargon. If you want to avoid management-speak and page-filling waffle, this book is definitely for you. Like all books in the series, *Influence and Succeed!* has been written in the belief that you can learn all you really need to know quickly and without fuss. The aim is to provide essential, practical advice that you can use straight away.

About the author

Fiona Elsa Dent is a faculty member at Ashridge Management College where she directs and tutors on the Influencing Strategies and Skills programme and the Developing Business and Leadership skills programme. In her role as trainer and coach she helps people develop a wide range of personal, interpersonal and relationship skills. Contact her at Fiona.Dent @ashridge.org.uk

Author's note

My motivation and inspiration to write this short book came from the managers and participants on the hundreds of training courses on which I have worked over my 20 years as a trainer and developer. Many of them wanted tips and techniques to help them become a better influencer. A number of the quotes used throughout this book come from these participants, but I have changed people's names to maintain their anonymity.

My colleagues at Ashridge (they know who they are) who work with me on the Influencing Strategies and Skills programme have helped and frequently contributed to the ideas and processes suggested in this book.

Good luck!

What's in this chapter for you

Influencing in business today
Why is influencing important?
What is influencing anyway?
What's in it for you and your business

" *Why can't they understand, I've done all the research,
I've presented the pros and cons, the case is rational and
factual and still they won't support my ideas.* "
– Richard Williams, quality manager

" *I don't get it. Why can't people just accept that I know how
things work around here? They always want to have a say and
they get all emotional when I suggest even the slightest little change.
Everything seems to be about compromise these days.* "
– Sylvia Brown, health and safety manager

Have you ever felt like this? What type of influencing
situations do you find frustrating or challenging?

Influencing in business today

In today's fast changing business environment there is an
increasing demand for people who can effectively influence others
for long-term results. Gone are the days of the boss who can rely
on their position in the hierarchy, their technical knowledge or
their ability to put forward an objective and rational case in order
to influence others.

" *The new kind of business hero must learn to operate without the
might of the hierarchy behind them. The crutch of authority must be
thrown away and replaced by their own ability to make relationships,
use influence and work with others to achieve results.* "
– Rosabeth Moss Kanter in *When Giants Learn To Dance*

Organisations and the people who work in them today have been:

- ○ delayered
- ○ downsized
- ○ flattened
- ○ empowered
- ○ re-engineered

to name but a few of the "management trends" to hit businesses and organisations worldwide.

The reality for many of you is that you will be working in an environment where project work and teamwork are common. These teams can often be multi-national and also cross-functional. All these things make their own challenges for you and your ability to influence.

Technological advances such as email, use of the internet, voicemail and videoconferencing all have to be assimilated into our daily routines and work practices, so change is becoming a norm and indeed you may feel that today much more is expected of you than ever before.

You might find it useful to reflect on your business environment and focus on the working practices which are common today, especially those which have an effect on your ability to influence others.

Why is influencing important?

❝ *So many situations I find myself in today involve me in influencing others. Business meetings, presentations, interviews and even family discussions.* ❞
– Gordon Murray, engineering consultant

Make a list of the influencing situations you find yourself in on a day-to-day basis. List them under business and social – you may wish to refer back to this list later in the book.

The ability to influence effectively is regarded by many as a key skill to develop and may contribute enormously to your achieving successful outcomes in the many face-to-face situations you find yourself in every day. Not only is skill in influencing necessary in your business life but it can also be very useful in both social and family situations, so perhaps working on your influencing can even help you to get your partner to go with you on that holiday of your dreams!

> ❝ *The new managerial role moves away from control and authority toward interdependence and participation.* ❞
> **– Anon**

The managerial role in today's business environment has changed, as has the roles of employees. Expectations are higher, people are better educated and there is emphasis on "working to live" rather than "living to work"! Participative management approaches, teamworking, globalisation and many of the other changes you face require new rules. More discussion, openness, sharing, trust and networking mean that the days of telling others what to do are gone and have been replaced by the need to influence others positively.

> ❝ *In today's turbulent business environment I truly believe that the skill to influence others positively has helped me enormously to build a good team, a wide customer base and to develop effective relationships with my suppliers.* ❞
> **– Sam Campbell, managing director of a computer software business**

What is influencing anyway?

> How would you define influencing? Think about the various situations you have been in where you think you have influenced someone successfully. What did you do, how did you go about it, what was the process?

There are many different definitions of influencing. Some are quite simple and others more complex.

" ... the ability to affect another's attitudes, beliefs or behaviours – seen only in its effect – without using coercion or formal position, and in such a way that influencees are acting in their own best interests. "

– E. Zuker in *The Seven Secrets Of Influence*

" Influence is what you achieve by using your power. It's about getting things done through other people. Influence implies the cabability to change other people's behaviour patterns and the decisions they take, or otherwise to affect events without actually having the power to do so. It is the art of getting the donkey to run or stop without using the stick. "

– Lee Bryce in *The Influential Manager*

" Influence is an active process whereby one person or group modifies the attitudes or behaviour of another person or group by adapting their behaviour and communication style in order to gain agreement and commitment to ideas and action. "

– Anon

Although there is no single commonly agreed definition of influencing the common themes in most definitions are:

○ moral use of power
○ working with others
○ commitment
○ cooperation
○ achieving effective outcomes for all
○ getting people on board.

Think of a time when you have recently been influenced by someone. What approaches did they use to get you on board?

What's in it for you and your business?

Why should you bother to develop your influencing skills? How will it help you in your career and in life?

In organisations where people have developed and use good influencing skills everyone will benefit because:

○ everyone will have the flexibility to cope with change
○ there will generally be a higher level of morale among staff
○ people will delegate more
○ teamworking will be more effective
○ bosses will generate less criticism and resistance from their staff due to greater involvement of all
○ all staff will have a better chance of attaining their goals and targets due to better use of all resources available
○ all people will feel empowered.

Think about your own place of work. Are you encouraged to use your influencing skills to get things done? If so, what benefits can you see? How does it affect your working environment?

At a personal level developing and using your skills of influence in a positive way will benefit you by:

○ raising your levels of self-confidence
○ giving you the ability to manage change more effectively
○ raising your personal credibility with others
○ developing your ability to involve others and gain their commitment
○ increasing your networks of contacts
○ enabling you to gain respect from colleagues
○ making you more effective and successful in your job and life.

❝ To be persuasive we must be believable; to be believable we must be credible; to be credible we must be truthful. ❞
– Edward R. Murrow

Now a few words about using influence in a negative or manipulative way. This type of influencing does not show respect for other people and implies that you are intending to exploit a situation or person for your own advantage. All influencing is about trying to get others to do what you want; the difference lies in the skills used. Manipulation uses spurious logic, power games, poor communication skills and generally shows little respect for the feelings of others. On the other hand, influencing shows respect for other people and is based on using openness and honesty to gain their commitment to your ideas.

The Prince by Machiavelli is perhaps the best known example of a text that tells of the effects of using manipulation on others.

> **Think about a time when you felt manipulated by someone. How did it make you feel? How did it affect the way you did your work? How did it affect your relationship with the other person?**

> ❝ *I used to work in an organisation where people didn't listen to each other and bosses used their power to influence us to do things their way. I always felt used and manipulated. I didn't stay with that company long and decided that after that experience I would never treat my staff or colleagues with such disrespect.* ❞
>
> **– Sam Campbell**

Influencing for short-term gain is something you all probably do from time to time. For instance, I regularly attempt to influence my teenage children to keep their bedrooms tidy. I have great success with this as a one-off but only when I (mis)use my power over them by withholding resources (pocket money, chauffeuring services, clean laundry, etc.). Why can't I get them to do it all the time? Perhaps there are just some things in this life that are not worth the hassle. By the way, if you have an answer to my problem please do let me know!

Misuse of power on a regular basis will result in the person you are influencing feeling that they have been manipulated, leading to mistrust, fear and loss of credibility and respect. The major point to remember is that truly successful influencers gain long-term commitment to their goals and outcomes.

Why should you develop your influencing?

You should now understand why influencing is important for you and have some ideas about your own influencing skills.

1. Influencing is about dealing with change and, let's face it, change is probably the only certainty in life today! What changes are facing you in your life at the moment?

2. Successful influencing will help you not only deal with change but also promote change in a positive way. Think about a change you are currently facing. How will you go about influencing others to accept and buy into the change?

3. Influencing will help you to effectively work with and through others. Getting others on board with your ideas is vital for successful influencing. How do you go about it?

4. Influencing is a key skill for getting the most out of many face-to-face situations you encounter. Think of all the face-to-face situations you deal with where influencing is a necessity.

5. Influencing skills are helpful not only in your working life but also in managing many of your relationships in your personal and social lives. How do you influence your friends and loved ones? Is this different to your business relationships?

6. Having influence and using your influencing skills effectively will enable you to raise your self-confidence, gain credibility with others and develop awareness of yourself and others. How else might it help you in your life?

What's in this chapter for you

Communication is the key
Skills for influencing
Qualities necessary for successful influencing

Communication is the key

Influencing successfully is predominantly about communication.
It involves developing and using a range of skills and abilities in
order to ensure that you are able to vary your approach to suit the
particular environment, people and situation.

Think about some of the communication skills that you use
when influencing. List them. Now reflect on how successful/
unsuccessful they are for you.

As well as communicating effectively, you must be understood and
for successful influencing to take place you have to have your
ideas accepted by the others involved.

> ❝ *Communication is not only about how well we say things
> but is about how well we are understood!* ❞
> **– Sam Campbell**

Have you ever had any of the following thoughts when you
have been attempting to influence other people?

❑ Why are they being so obtuse?
❑ Why can't they just understand?
❑ Why do they have to ask so many questions?
❑ Why are they so difficult?

If these questions relate to you then it is highly likely that although you are getting your ideas across you are probably not doing it in the most efficient way. You might be successful in the end, but it may be a more tortuous process than necessary.

When communicating, and particularly when attempting to influence others, understanding the impact of what you are saying on the other people is essential. Research (Mehrabian 1972) has shown that of the impact of your communication:

- ○ **7% depends on what is actually said**
- ○ **38% depends on how you actually speak**
- ○ **55% depends on how you look and behave.**

This suggests that a staggering 93% of what we are trying to communicate to others is non-verbal. This does not mean that the words you use are unimportant, indeed one of the necessary skills for influencing is verbal fluency, but "non-verbal communication" is equally important – perhaps even more important bearing in mind the above statistics.

Try this experiment out on a few close friends or colleagues.
- ❑ Think of a sentence that you can say in several different ways in order to convey different meanings (by putting different emphasis on different words each time) – for instance, "I'd like a word with you".
- ❑ Now try saying it again using non-verbal communication to convey different meanings, e.g. anger, friendliness, inquisitiveness, etc.
- ❑ Ask them how they felt about the way you were saying the sentence. What does this tell you about the necessity for clarity and impact on the way you use your communication skills?

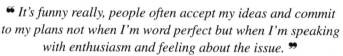

> ❝ *It's funny really, people often accept my ideas and commit to my plans not when I'm word perfect but when I'm speaking with enthusiasm and feeling about the issue.* ❞
> **– Sylvia Brown**

Skills for influencing

Effective influencers recognise that in order to become successful you have to develop a range of skills and in order to remain successful you have to continue to build on these skills.

Six of the most important skills are:

- ○ active listening
- ○ verbal fluency
- ○ awareness of body language
- ○ visioning
- ○ planning
- ○ preparation.

Active listening

Active listening is a much more complex process than most of us realise. It is not simply using your ears; it involves taking a participative part in any dialogue between people.

> 66 *I'll not listen to reason. Reason always means what someone else has got to say.* 99
> **– E. C. Gaskell, British writer**

> 66 *The important thing is not to stop questioning. Curiosity has its own reason for existing.* 99
> **– Albert Einstein**

Active listening involves a range of skills including:

- ○ questioning
- ○ probing
- ○ testing understanding
- ○ summarising
- ○ displaying supportive body language.

> 66 *Seek first to understand then to be understood.* 99
> **– Stephen Covey, in *Seven Habits Of Highly Effective People***

Active listening involves listening and questioning – probing and testing understanding in order to get a full understanding of the issue under discussion. The truly effective influencer will spend much time doing this before they even attempt to begin actively influencing others. Listening actively to others by displaying a range of both non-verbal and verbal communication techniques has the effect of showing others you respect their views and ideas and helps you to gain credibility and respect.

> **❝** *Remember it is important to consider both the human and the hidden factors.* **❞**
> **– Hilda Dent, retired hospital matron (my mother in law!)**

An additional benefit of active listening is that you begin to understand the other person's perspective on the issue, thus enabling you to prepare your case accordingly, perhaps by incorporating their ideas into a shared solution.

List three people you know whom you would regard as highly effective listeners and make a note of why this is.

Verbal fluency

Influencing almost always involves you in a dialogue where you have to articulate your ideas to others. This involves you in thinking about:

○ the language you will use
○ the linguistic techniques you will employ when speaking
○ pace
○ emphasis
○ intonation
○ the approach to take
○ the audience – one-to-one, a meeting or a formal presentation.

In terms of the language or words remember that it is important to ensure you choose to use words that express what you want to say rather than to impress people. Also remember that, to paraphrase the song, "it's not what you say but the way that you say it".

❝ *I believe that precision with words is far less important than the energy, passion and enthusiasm I use to convey them.* ❞

– Michael White

Think of a famous person or TV personality whom you admire for their qualities as an effective speaker. Next time you see or hear them speak listen to the words they use and the way they use their voice to get their message across. What can you learn from this to help in your influencing discussions?

Awareness of body language

Your non-verbal messages, and in particular your body language, play a crucial role in how you are perceived and understood by others. However, before looking at body language in more detail I would like to ring a warning bell. It is very easy to stereotype here: all people who fold their arms are being defensive; or people who touch their ear are telling lies. It might be that folding your arms is comfortable listening behaviour and as for the ear it could just be itchy!

Here are a few important points to remember about body language:

- ○ First impressions are often based on body language and non-verbal communication.
- ○ Within a few seconds your listener will be making judgements about you.
- ○ Be aware of your own body language and the message you wish to convey to others.
- ○ When observing others' body language look for clusters of behaviour and not just single gestures.
- ○ Try to check out any cues and clues you are picking up – ask them!

Have you ever suddenly realised that your first impression of someone was completely wrong? What changed your mind? Was it easy or difficult?

You might also like to consider the saying "You don't get a second chance to make a first impression!"

Think about when you meet someone for the first time. How do you make those all-important first impressions?

The most powerful non-verbal signals are conveyed by:

○ facial expression
○ eye contact
○ posture
○ gestures
○ appearance (dress)
○ touch, including handshake.

When you are in discussion with others, or at a meeting or giving a presentation, what body language do you use? What impression does it give to others? You may have to ask others for their feedback here. Make a list of the things that are positive impressions and those that are not so positive.

Visioning

Much has been written about the process and importance of visioning. I believe that there is no other situation in which it is more important than when you are attempting to influence others. Visioning is not just for boards of directors, or big organisations; you too should be able to visualise where you want to go and how you want to get there.

> ❝ *A vision gives meaning and purpose to your actions.*
> *It is the picture on the jigsaw box of life!* ❞
>
> **– Anon**

Visioning is simply about communicating effectively. It involves:

○ verbally painting a picture of where you want to go (visual aids can of course help here)
○ describing your ideal outcome

○ keeping it simple and buyable into
○ showing enthusiasm
○ using images, metaphors, analogies and stories
○ focusing on the future.

One example of visioning can be seen in the movie *Braveheart*, where the Scots are about to go into battle with the English. They are having second thoughts until William Wallace (Mel Gibson in disguise!) rides up with his supporters. At this point he makes a very moving speech ending with the words "they may take our lives, but they'll never take our freedom!"

You don't have to be William Wallace (or Mel Gibson for that matter) to be able to vision. Anyone can do it, although posses-sion of commitment, enthusiasm and courage will help.

Try this. Focus on an important issue you would like to influence others about. How might you present it to them in terms of a vision. What is your vision and what aids might you need to help?

The two other skills which are vital for success when influencing are planning and preparation. They are so important I have devoted a whole chapter to each of them!

1. Communication is the key to successful influencing. Develop your communication skills so your ideas will be both understood and accepted.
2. Understanding the impact you are making on others is vital so focus on what you are going to do to make it. Think about what you'll say, how you'll say it and what you'll be doing when you say it.
3. Listen actively to understand others by asking questions, probing, testing understanding and summarising. Awareness of others and their views is essential.
4. Ensure fluent articulation of your ideas but always with a clear focus on the particular audience you are addressing at the time.
5. Non-verbal communication has a major effect on your message and how you are perceived, so think about your body language and how you will use your voice.
6. Creating a vision of the future by focusing on the outcome you desire can be a powerful way of gaining and retaining people's attention.

Qualities necessary for successful influencing

> Do you ever find yourself thinking "If only I could be as confident as ...!" or "Why can't my ideas come across with such oomph?"

Perhaps one of the reasons for this might be that in addition to the skills you need to develop there are also several qualities that will help you to be both effective and successful. They are:

- ○ self-confidence
- ○ adaptability and flexibility
- ○ enthusiasm
- ○ patience
- ○ credibility
- ○ courage.

There is no denying that these qualities are difficult to develop. Some would say that you can't develop them because they are inherent. Perhaps some of the above do come more naturally to some people than to others, but I believe that all of these qualities can be developed and used by everyone. What do they all involve and mean?

> Take a few moments now to make two lists. List the qualities you believe you possess that help when you are influencing and then list the qualities you think you need to work on.

Self-confidence

Self-confidence involves having a belief in yourself and in your influencing. It involves being self-aware about your particular skills and abilities as well as having an understanding of your weaknesses and development needs.

Who do you regard as self-confident? Think about people who you know personally as well as famous people. List them and then think about what it is that they do to convey this self-confidence. Why not ask the people on the list that you know how they feel about their own self-confidence? You may be surprised by their response!

There are numerous examples of famous people who appear to be supremely self-confident when in the public eye but are full of self-doubt and fear when away from the camera. Just think of how many famous people end up in clinics dealing with their alchohol or drug abuse!

Read some biographies of famous people. These are often very insightful and can help you to understand more about self-confidence, what it is, what it means and how to develop it.

I had an interesting experience several years ago when I was a Management Development Manager in a financial services company. The incident remains with me until this day and taught me more about self-confidence than any book. I was relatively new to the organisation and about three months into the job at the time. I'd been running quite a few short seminars and meetings with various managers and supervisors attempting to influence them about the importance of developing themselves and their people. A young woman who was a supervisor in the organisation came up to me after one of the seminars and said, "I would like to be as confident and assertive as you are. Can you run a course that will help me develop these skills?"

Two things struck me about this. Firstly she had no idea about how nervous and frightened I felt inside and secondly I had regarded her as one of the more self-confident women managers in the organisation!

This experience taught me that much of life is about perception and how you come across to others. In order to understand how you are perceived you have to ask for feedback from others. Very often this will give you the biggest and most effective boost to your self-confidence.

Adaptability and flexibility

The ability to change and adapt to different situations is vital for successful influencing. The skilled influencer realises that there is no single correct way to influence. There are only effective skills and qualities that can help you in the process. The success of any influencing interaction is often down to how these skills and qualities are used in practice. Adaptability and flexibility are the key; they enable you to vary your style and approach to suit the situation and people involved.

In many instances people are much more likely to accept your ideas and come on board with you if they feel that you are listening to them and taking account of their views as well, and then subsequently adapting your plans accordingly.

> ❝ *When I first started in marketing as a young graduate trainee I used to go into product meetings all guns blazing, thinking my ideas were unique and right all the time. Over time I began to realise that not only was I sometimes wrong but that I often upset people with my attitude. I began to realise that I had to cool off, be more flexible, vary my approach and sometimes I had to compromise and accept that others had good ideas about my products as well.* ❞
> **– Michael White, marketing director**

> When was the last time you had to adapt your ideas and compromise on an issue? How did it make you feel? How did it make the others involved feel?

Enthusiasm

I've always felt that if you cannot be enthusiastic about your subject how on earth can you expect others to be! Enthusiasm is something you show in your behaviour and in your voice. It is always very easy to detect your lack of commitment to a subject by your lack of enthusiasm in your presentation of it.

Think about the last time that you were with friends and you were all discussing a shared interest or hobby, something you are all passionate about. What was the atmosphere like? How were you talking? What was the general feeling in the room like?

Typically some or all of the following demonstrate enthusiasm:

○ variation in vocal tone
○ speed of speech – make it pacy and upbeat
○ use of stories and anecdotes
○ varied facial expression – smiles in particular
○ expansive gestures
○ eye contact
○ vivid and expressive language.

> **"** *Nothing great was ever achieved without enthusiasm and commitment.* **"**
>
> **– Anon**

Patience

Have you ever thought "If only I'd waited, bided my time and chosen the right moment rather than diving straight in"?

It is said that patience is a virtue, and this is no more so than when you are attempting to influence others. Influencing effectively involves so many different people, environments and situations that it is not something to be rushed. Having the patience and persistence to stay with your issue and not give up will be quite a challenge, but it will pay dividends in the long run.

Preparing to influence others can take you days, weeks and even months of careful planning and discussion. The truly effective influencer takes time to prepare the case, does the research and networks with others to assess their position on the issue.

> **"** *I'm quite an impatient person, I want things to happen straight away. This is difficult in my job because everyone wants to have*

their say, so I've had to learn to be more patient, to involve others and listen to their point of view. I'm beginning to find that this can be really helpful to my cause especially when I find many more people on my side than I thought. **"**
– Sylvia Brown, health and safety manager

Credibility

Credibility has to be earned and it doesn't come easily. Typically it is based on people's perceptions of you and on your history. Prior success, knowledge and expertise in an area all help to establish your credibility but this is not sufficient. Developing honest, open and trusting relationships with others is also vital.

Credibility earns you a first hearing. It gives you the opportunity to start talking to others about your ideas, but in order to keep them listening and talking you must maintain their trust by showing that you are consistent. Research has shown that the most consistently successful influencers have a track record in terms of their knowledge, skills and ability to work in the best interests of others.

Evaluate you own credibility by reviewing your track record. Consider:

❏ your knowledge and expertise
❏ previous success when influencing
❏ the type of relationship you have with the other stakeholders
❏ how you are regarded by them.

Having done this you could try asking a couple of colleagues how they perceive you in these areas!

Courage

"If only I'd taken the chance, if only I'd risked it." "Why did I have to go for the safe option?" "Why didn't I follow my instinct?" Do these sound familiar?

> ❝ *Courage is about taking risks – not dangerous risks but calculated well thought through risks. It means sticking out your neck and standing up for what you believe in. This hasn't always been easy and I've ruffled a few feathers along the way, but I think it means people know where I'm coming from and what I believe in.* ❞
> **– Sam Campbell**

Courage involves bravery, it means having the guts to stand up and be counted and to commit to what you believe in. Courage where influencing is concerned involves taking risks, so if you:

- ○ **know your subject**
- ○ **do your research**
- ○ **prepare and plan**
- ○ **involve others**

you won't be taking a dangerous risk but simply a calculated one, you'll know where others stand, you'll understand how much of a challenge you face and above all you will instinctively know if it's worth the risk at all.

You may find that development of the skills mentioned at the beginning of this section will contribute to your ability to demonstrate and use the qualities listed.

The lists of skills and qualities for influencing are not meant to be exhaustive. I am sure you will be able to add to them. However, in my opinion they do cover some of those regarded as most important for effective and successful influencing.

1. Ask others for feedback on how you come across when you are influencing. In particular ask them to concentrate on what they see as your strengths and weaknesses.
2. Being self-aware and having self-belief lead to self-confidence, which is a valuable quality for influencing successfully.
3. Compromise and variation of your influencing approach, showing adaptability to others, helps show that there is no one correct answer but simply different ways to get to the best outcome for all.
4. Enthusiasm can be more important than any other quality. Lack of it easily leads to failure.

5. Having the persistence to stick with your ideas and having the patience to plan and prepare effectively will reap rewards in the long term.

6. Establishing your credibility by being regarded by others as trustworthy, open and honest will ensure that people give you a fair hearing.

7. Taking calculated risks and having the courage of your own convictions will be quite a challenge, but if you truly believe in something is it really that risky?

What's in this chapter for you

Your influencing network
Stakeholder mapping
Knowing your subject

> "If only I'd thought that through a little longer." "I should have anticipated that reaction." "If only I'd spent a little longer planning." If you can relate to any of these statements then lack of planning might be your problem.

Time spent planning is never wasted. Planning effectively and thoroughly will help you enormously. Some of the benefits to you are that you will:

- ○ anticipate and plan for problem areas and people
- ○ understand all the stakeholders and their perspectives
- ○ plan how to deal with emotion
- ○ have a thorough knowledge of you topic/issue
- ○ develop networks with others to help in your influencing process
- ○ establish your credentials and expertise about your issue
- ○ feel more self-confident during the whole process.

Remember the 6Ps

Proper Prior Planning Promotes Peak Performance

Or put another way

Proper Prior Planning Prevents Poor Performance!

So, what can you do to plan? The following tips focus on two key areas which are vital for success in effective influencing: the people and the subject/issue.

Your influencing network

> *Most of the time I know the people that I am influencing,
> so when I experience a problem I could kick myself that I haven't
> spent enough time planning and preparing.*
>
> **– Sylvia Brown**

Awareness and knowledge about the people that you have to
influence on a regular basis is a great starting point for planning.
Most of you will have a limited network of people whom you have
to influence and typically these people will fall into one of the
following categories:

- bosses
- colleagues
- direct reports
- customers
- suppliers
- friends
- family

For some of these categories you will be able to identify particular
people by name. For others it will be sufficient to categorise them
by type. The important point is to be aware of the people you
have to influence. This will enable you to use all your experiences
of relating to the person as opportunities for gathering information
about them. This information can then be made use of when you
are more directly involved in an influencing discussion.

> Take a sheet of paper or a notebook and make a list or
> perhaps draw a mind map of everybody in your influencing
> network. Start by listing the categories of people. Then if
> appropriate add people's names so you have the full picture
> of your influencing network. In addition you may like to note
> beside the names/categories information which you feel
> might be useful for influencing them in the future.

Stakeholder mapping

This simple planning tool involves focusing on the particular
influencing issue that you are facing at any one moment and is
really a subset of your influencing network.

In this context a stakeholder is any person who has an involvement in the result and process of your influencing goal. The mapping bit is the picture you draw listing all those who have an interest, involvement or stake in your issue.

Take a sheet of paper and write down your influencing goal in the centre. Then add branches around this goal, labelling each branch with either a category or the actual name of the stakeholder.

Having completed this picture you should now be well aware of all the stakeholders you have to influence, and assuming you prepare this well in advance of any influencing discussion, you will be able to add names to it during your planning phase.

The real value in the stakeholder map however, is not simply the picture of the names but the information about the people that you can add to this picture.

The sort of information you should be collecting about the people on your stakeholder map is:

○ the high and low influencers in their own right
○ who supports and who is against your issue
○ the behaviour and approaches that turn them on and off
○ the winners and losers regarding your influencing issue
○ the approach they typically use when influencing you
○ the power they have to influence the situation.

Having done this type of detailed analysis of all the people involved you will have a much clearer picture of the influencing challenge that faces you.

> **❝** *Stakeholder mapping is such a simple idea, I just wish I'd known about it years ago. I'm sure it's going to save me loads of time and effort in the future.* **❞**
> **– Jim Wilson, customer service manager**

There are many reasons for failing to influence. Some of the most common include:

○ making assumptions about the people involved
○ making assumptions about the decision makers

○ not recognising one or two of the key stakeholders
○ failing to understand the position of some of your
   stakeholders.

Preparing a stakeholder map and the subsequent thorough
analysis of this map can help you to avoid some or possibly all of
these problems.

Knowing your subject

Having detailed knowledge and experience of your subject would
seem like common sense. However, you know what they say
about common sense: it's not very common!

Having a thorough understanding of the whole topic area is
probably the most important advantage you can give yourself. It
may be worth taking heed of the saying "Knowledge is power".

For many of you, in your working environment anyway, you will
be influencing others on a limited range of topics probably related
to your day-to-day work, so having an in-depth knowledge and
understanding of the area is vital for successful influencing. As
well as your own knowledge and experience you would be well
advised to have some insight into the historical context of your
issue and others views on it both inside and outside your
organisation.

Focus now on an issue where you have recently had success
when influencing others. Reflect on your knowledge,
understanding and experience of this topic. How would
others regard your knowledge and experience in this area?

There are certain disadvantages associated with knowledge,
especially with over-dependence on knowledge alone. For
instance:

○ over-complicating a subject for some of your stakeholders
○ appearing arrogant about your knowledge and expertise
○ not listening to others' points of view
○ regarding yourself as the expert and thus discarding the views
   of others who are less knowledgeable.

" *Knowledge is a treasure, but practice is the key to it.* "
– Proverb

Knowledge alone is not enough. Experience of working with that knowledge is what makes you a successful influencer. The two used together will raise your self-confidence and your credibility with others.

Keeping up-to-date, developing and extending your knowledge, are also useful for influencing others. Here are some ideas.

- ○ Read relevant literature, especially books and journals.
- ○ Read a good quality daily newspaper.
- ○ Talk to other "experts" both in and out of your organisation.
- ○ Network with others at conferences, professional organisations, etc.

Planning is the key

" *Plans are nothing: planning is everything.* "
– Dwight D. Eisenhower

Getting the planning phase right, no matter how long you spend on it, will pay dividends in the long run. Plans help to get you focused on where you are going. Effective planning forces you to consider your plans from many aspects and enables you to build in contingencies should they be necessary.

Having a structured approach to your planning will help you to deal with any unforeseen barriers or challenges that you come up against. A good plan with sufficient planning behind it will enable you to be flexible and to adapt and modify your actions, yet still reach your desired outcome.

In the words of the Scottish poet Robert Burns,

" *The best laid plans O' mice an' men gang aft a-gley!* "
– Robert Burns

1. Plan planning into your schedule! Never skimp on the time necessary for planning. Time spent on this phase of your influencing will reward you richly in the long run.

2. Having a thorough understanding of the people involved and your subject will raise your self-confidence when influencing others.

3. Focus on your influencing network by identifying the people you have to influence most often.

4. When you have identified all the people in your influencing network make notes about information that will assist you when influencing them in the future.

5. Use stakeholder mapping as a simple planning tool. Focus on an influencing issue facing you now and draw a stakeholder map detailing all the people involved.

6. Analyse your stakeholder map by annotating it with relevant information, which will assist you when you begin to plan your actual influencing strategy and approach.

7. To influence effectively you need to know your subject inside out so keep yourself up-to-date.

8. Knowledge is not enough. You must demonstrate to others through your day-to-day actions that you are both knowledgeable and experienced in the area.

What's in this chapter for you

Understanding influencing style
Influencing approaches
Tactics to choose from
The role of power in influencing
Influencing and technology

At this stage you are now beginning to get down to the nitty gritty of the influencing process. You should have:

○ thought about your own position
○ focused on your particular skills and weaknesses when influencing
○ explored the context of the situation
○ thought about the position of all the others involved
○ drawn and analysed your stakeholder map
○ acquired a thorough knowledge of your subject.

You are now in a position to start preparing how you will actually go about the interactive process.

> ❝ *This is the bit I always find most difficult. Having done so much work in the planning and analysing phases it is very easy to just go for it and jump in feet first. In many ways preparing the detail of how I will influence the different people is the most important phase of all.* ❞
>
> **– Jim Wilson**

At this point it might be worth mentioning the old but valuable adage: to fail to prepare is to prepare to fail!

How often recently have you come away from a dialogue with someone else thinking that perhaps a little more detailed thinking about how you were going to manage the discussion would have helped?

Understanding influencing style

Most of us have a preferred influencing style. This means that typically you will adopt a preferred range of behaviours and skills in order to get your point across. This preferred style will have developed over many years and will usually be based on your previous success in using the skills and behaviours. However, using one style for all situations and people is probably not the most efficient path to successful influencing.

> **Think about some recent influencing discussions you have had where getting your ideas across has been more challenging than you thought it would be; where you've been failing to get the others to buy in. What did you have to do to get their commitment? Often a slight change of style or approach is all that is necessary.**

Influencing style and adaptation of it is not about changing your personality; it is simply about your levels of awareness, adaptability and flexibility. Let's look at one way of defining of your influencing style that should help you to prepare more effectively for your influencing discussions. Look at the three different descriptions below and try to identify your own preference.

	People oriented	Analytical	Outcome-focused
General description of each type	Want to work with people to help them develop and be responsive to their needs	Want to have the opportunity to think things through and to analyse issues before deciding.	Want to get things done, happy to take the lead, to compete and take risks.
Typical behaviours and approaches used to influence	• Involving others • Questioning and listening • Friendly and open • Sincere • Chatty and discussive	• High level of detail • Thorough • Factual • Risk free • Logical and clear	• Assertive • Outcome-focused • Challenging • Innovative • Verbally fluent and confident
How you like to be influenced	• Be needed • Be valued • Have your ideas considered • Asked and involved	• Time to think • Not rushed • Safe, well researched options • Presented in a logical, factual and structured way	• Opportunity to lead • High profile project • Something new and novel • Links to your own goals

Are you someone who is predominantly people-oriented, analytical or outcome-focused?

> " *I know I'm an analytical type. I like to present all the facts and figures and let them speak for themselves. I always do my research and in my own mind I know I'm putting forward the best options for everyone. Sometimes I find this approach lets me down because other people can be more concerned about how my plans will affect their staff and about the implementation procedures. It baffles me because I do consider all the people yet I am sometimes accused of being too hard.* "
> **– Sylvia Brown, health and safety manager**

This quote is fairly typical for many people, yet it is simple to overcome. Often our strength in putting together our case using our preferred style can turn into a weakness when preparing to influence others. Remember that in order to influence effectively you must:

○ **plan and prepare thoroughly**
○ **put yourself in the other people's shoes.**

Knowing your own preference is one thing but the real skill is in your ability to vary your particular influencing style to suit the people you are influencing at the time. If you are one-to-one this means focusing on the other person's particular needs. If you are in a group then you should assume that there will probably be people of each type in the audience and prepare accordingly. So think also about the people that you plan to influence and ask yourself which style might be used to influence them. Might it involve a combination of several with no over reliance on one particular style?

Influencing approaches

Focusing on the approach you choose to use relates more to the tone you wish to take when influencing. This can be addressed in the following two ways:

	Assertive approach – tell	Involving approach – sell
Typical behaviours used	• Verbal fluency • Logical and objective • Clear and determined • Persistence • Focused on the outcome	• Listens and questions • Uses "we" • Looks for commitment and involvement • Appeals to others' imagination
Typical situations when appropriate	• When time is of the essence • Routine issues • When you are clear about the outcome you want • When safety is an issue • When there is only one answer (sometimes this is the case!)	• When a joint solution is needed • When you need full commitment from the others involved • Long-term team or project work • When you need ideas from others

You can sometimes get hooked on one approach more than another. Each of the styles and approaches mentioned above has advantages and disadvantages and there is no one style that will work all the time. In fact overuse or dependence on one particular style will tend in the long run to work against you. To be a truly successful influencer you should adapt and adjust your style and approach to suit the people and the situation you are faced with.

Examine the two tables above and try to identify your own preferred influencing style. Now identify situations when your style has worked well for you. Analyse why this is. When has it not worked so well? Why might this be?

Tactics to choose from

Tactics can sound a little Machiavellian, implying using "unfair tactics". However in this context I view tactics simply as additional tools you may choose to use when influencing. While you are preparing your influencing strategy you must focus not only on the skills, style and approaches you will use but also on the tactic.

○ **Emotion – appealing to the feelings, values and beliefs of the person or people you are influencing, and showing your own** emotions while doing so. Emotion is a powerful influencing ally and many would say the inability to show emotion when influencing today is a major disadvantage. However, take care not to overdo it as some people may feel they are being blackmailed emotionally!

○ Coercion – when you use insistence or pressure to influence others. Often this particular tactic depends on your position and power base. If it is used you must take care as it can lead to resentment in others and almost certainly lack of trust and respect in the long run if over used.

○ Reason – probably the most common tactic among business people today and the basis of many influencing discussions. Reason involves you in putting forward a rational, logical and well thought through case. However, research has shown that reason alone is probably not sufficient as decision-making is not always rational and objective.

○ Compromise – this tactic is often used when it is recognised that a little give and take is necessary. You must work together to negotiate an effective and satisfactory outcome for all stakeholders. Success in using this tactic depends on your use of good communication skills and acceptance in the first place that your way is not the only way.

○ Participation – this means sharing in the whole process and is about mutual agreement. Effective use of this tactic can be very time consuming and demands a great deal of mutual trust and respect. It involves encouraging other people to develop their own analysis and solutions to the issue. If time allows, this tactic generates a high level of commitment from all those involved.

○ Charisma – those of you lucky enough to have it can use your charm and persona to influence others. But beware – over dependence can appear manipulative.

○ Specialist – when you are an expert or have specialist information that is highly relevant to a situation. This is often useful where new ideas may be necessary to reach an effective outcome. Care of course must be taken when using this tactic in case you patronise the person or people you are influencing.

Reflect on the above list of tactics. Identify those that you use, and those that you need to develop. Thinking about a current influencing situation, which tactic/s will you use?

As with influencing style and approach you should try to identify those tactics you tend to over rely on and those you need to work on. Over reliance on any one tactic can become ineffective in the long term.

> ❝ *Peter's a real charmer. He can get the toughest of customers eating out of his hands. His only problem is that when you've been on the receiving end of his tactics for a while you begin to know that there is no reciprocity – he really only wants to get his own way!* ❞
>
> **– Jim Wilson**

How you use your tactics is down to you and as with all other aspects of influencing the important issue is to ensure a win–win for all involved! Trust, respect and honesty are the bedrock for successful influencers. It's not worth the risk to your reputation to even have the suggestion of a dirty tactic levelled at you!

The role of power in influencing

Power and the use of it are often regarded negatively in the context of influencing. Perhaps this has come about because of the way people use their power when influencing. Power suggests that you have the ability or authority to act in your own right. The power to make a decision on a particular issue because of your position in the hierarchy is called "position power". In the context of influencing, if you were to use your position power to continually tell people what to do you may be regarded as influential in that you can get people to do things, but would they do the same things for you if you did not have position power?

> ❝ *I've worked in a couple of organisations where bosses use their power to get things done. People like this don't seem to think we have ideas of our own and can help them to solve problems. They may think they're being influential but really they're just autocrats who gain little respect or commitment from me.* ❞
>
> **– Gordon Murray**

As we've already seen the successful and effective influencer wants to work with others to gain commitment and buy-in to outcomes. Having an awareness of the power bases you possess in any influencing situation is useful and as long as you use your power in an ethical way to assist in your goal then using your power can be a great support to you.

We all have certain power bases upon which we can draw and often these will vary from situation to situation. Some of the sources of our power are:

○ Position power – your position in the hierarchy
○ Resource power – access to and control of various resources, e.g. money, people, supplies, etc.
○ Network power – this is related to relationships and people you know who can help
○ Knowledge power – access to knowledge or information especially specialist knowledge
○ Expert power – having special skills that are in short supply in your organisation
○ Charismatic power – your personality, people want to follow you!
○ Visionary power – the ability to stand up for what you believe and to transmit that belief to others

Think of a recent influencing situation you have faced. Reflect on the above list of power sources. Which are appropriate for you? Did you use them? Were you aware of them? Can you think of any other power sources you have?

It is inevitable that each of you will have certain power bases that you can use when influencing others. Awareness of these power bases is valuable when planning your strategy and interactions, and it is also worth reflecting on the power sources of the person or people you are influencing. The important thing about power is not to abuse it, but to be aware of it and the clout it gives you when influencing. Used effectively power is a major benefit that will complement your influencing skills and approach.

> ❝ Early in my managerial career I was given a very sound piece of advice from one of my bosses – to never abuse any position of power I may attain because people have long memories and you never know where and when they will pop up in the future! ❞
> **– Michael White**

Influencing and technology

Technology has an impact on many aspects of our lives and influencing others is certainly not excluded from this. For instance some of the ways in which technology can affect you in an influencing context are:

○ influencing during telephone conversations
○ electronic mail messages
○ meetings via video conferencing
○ presentations using datashows.

The key problem with technology is probably our growing dependence on it. It cuts out the human touch that is so vitally important to the whole influencing process.

> ❝ *I'm growing to hate email. So many people seem to use it rather than talking to each other. It's so easy to be misunderstood on email. I know it has its place and it can be a great way of saving time but if an issue is important then surely its worth the time and energy to talk as well!* ❞
>
> **– Sylvia Brown**

Some of the specific problems associated with technology when influencing are:

○ inability to see people and their reactions
○ missing cues and clues which are predominantly based on other people's body language
○ under or over explaining and issue with email, thus making your message too terse or alternatively diluting it
○ misunderstanding someone's vocal tone on the telephone when it is out of synchronisation with the unseen body language
○ detracting or distracting from your key messages with datashow presentations, which appear to be easy, but need careful thought as to the content and structure of your visuals.

Preparation – some tips

Preparing your strategy for influencing is the most challenging task of all in order to be a successful influencer. Thoroughness at this stage is vital. Failure to prepare may not lead to total failure in the long run, but those of you who have failed to prepare sufficiently in the past will know how much more stressful it can make the whole process.

Remember the stakeholder map you drew for a current influencing issue? Go back to it and annotate it with the following information about each of the people or groups.

❑ What influencing style do they use?
❑ What style seems to work on them?
❑ What influencing approach do they use?
❑ What influencing tactics seem to work on them?
❑ What power bases do each of them have?

Now analyse the stakeholder map. What does it tell you about the way you should tackle each of them?

---

1. Be aware of and understand your own preferred style of influencing. Reflect on a few recent influencing situations and using the three typical styles try to assess which is your preferred one. So do you tend to be more people-oriented, are you analytical or do you prefer to be outcome-focused?
2. You might also find it useful to use the same categories to analyse the person or people you are influencing in order to determine how they prefer to be influenced. This can help you enormously when preparing your strategy.
3. The actual approach you take when influencing can be a matter of habit, but the situation and environment also usually affect it. So, are you an assertive teller or an involving seller? Which approach is the most appropriate?
4. The particular tactics you use when influencing others are important additions to your style and approach, but care should be taken lest they should be regarded as "dirty tactics" when overdone.
5. You all have certain power bases that you can draw upon. Ethical and principled use of power provides you with another resource to use when influencing others. Awareness of others' power bases is also useful when influencing as this can help you to choose the right approach and style.

6. Influencing is largely about relationship development and how you interact with others. The impact of technology on the whole area of relationship development is huge, so remember that influencing continues when you are on the telephone, email or video conferencing.

7. Allow yourself enough time for thorough and detailed preparation. You know this makes sense – too many of us skimp at this stage and regret it!

What's in this chapter for you

> *The influencing process*
> *Influencing – a model*
> *Understanding your influencing environment*
> *Raising self-awareness*
> *Understanding and analysing others*
> *Exploring skills and approaches*
> *Deciding on your influencing strategy*

What is it that makes you successful when influencing some people yet fail dismally with others? Why is it that when you are attempting to influence several people about a change some are easier than others?

The influencing process

We have already established that to influence successfully you need to do more than simply get your facts together, put forward a logical and rational case and talk to the relevant people. Influencing is in fact a long-term process, which involves:

○ developing relationships with others
○ establishing your own credibility
○ gaining the trust of others
○ having patience
○ preparing a well researched case
○ not necessarily being the expert but having good knowledge of the issue.

As well as all of the above it is important to realise that in influencing other people you must be willing to deal with emotion – your own and that of the others involved.

❝ *The heart has its reasons, which are quite unknown to the head.* ❞
– Blaise Pascal

Reflect on some recent influencing situations you have experienced, perhaps where you have had unexpected (to you anyway) responses from others.

❏   What emotions have been expressed, how, why?
❏   How did it make you feel and respond?

❝ *Once I began to understand that it wasn't just the facts that people wanted or needed, and that sometimes the response I get from others to my ideas was irrational and emotional, not because they couldn't see the logic behind the proposal but because their heart told them a different story, I began to realise that influencing was hard work, needing more than a one-off slug. I had to be more patient focusing on how I approach my colleagues as well as on the topic itself.* ❞
– Sylvia Brown

By adopting a more structured approach, and accepting that it may take longer than you want to get people on board you could significantly increase your success in influencing others. You might also find influencing to be more fun and certainly less stressful.

Influencing – a model

The model that follows suggests a process that will help you to plan and prepare for any influencing challenge you face. It is based on the premise that as an influencer you have to vary your skills, approach, tactics and behaviours to suit the environment, people and indeed the situation. The motto should be: "Different strokes for different folks".

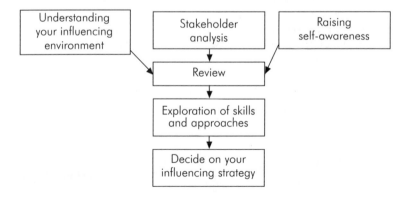

Focus on a recent real-life influencing issue you have had to deal with. Write down what your goal was and whether or not you reached a satisfactory outcome. As you work through the model focus on the same issue and apply the various stages to it.

Understanding your influencing environment

Understanding and awareness of your influencing environment is vital to your success. Whatever the environment, from a large organisation to a small family unit, understanding and being aware of what behaviour is acceptable and unacceptable are vital. In business this is sometimes known as the "culture" of the organisation. This idea can be applied to any type of organisation. The culture includes:

- ○ how people dress
- ○ how people address each other (first names?)
- ○ ways of working
- ○ written and unwritten rules
- ○ what happens at meetings
- ○ levels of formality.

In this context, culture can be defined as "the way we do things around here".

Think about the environment within which you are attempting to influence others. What are the unwritten rules that you instinctively know have to be adhered to? Make a list of these. This list should help you understand the culture and what behaviours might work and which wouldn't work. List these behaviours. They will be useful later.

Raising self-awareness

This means understanding yourself, your values and beliefs, your strengths and weaknesses, likes and dislikes as well as your preferred approach when relating to others. Raising your level of self-awareness will help you enormously when deciding on the appropriate approaches and tactics to use when influencing others.

ACT!

Make some notes about yourself. Use the following headings and in each case try to list at least five examples:

❑ My key strengths are . . .
❑ My worst weaknesses are . . .
❑ The things I like doing best are . . .
❑ The things I dislike doing most are . . .
❑ The things I most value in life are . . .
❑ My most important beliefs about this issue are . . .
❑ The behaviours, skills and approaches I use most when influencing others are . . .

Now examine this list for any key messages or patterns.

❝ *Taking time out to really think about myself and how I related to other people in my day-to-day discussions helped me understand that not everyone was like me – we all have different ways of doing things. More than anything else this has helped me to understand the complexity of the influencing process.* ❞
– Richard Williams, quality manager

You are all very different personalities, yet you all develop preferred ways of working and interacting. These behaviours have been learned over many years and are usually based on what has worked for us in the past. Typically this means that when faced with the many challenges of daily life you automatically deal with them using your preferred range of behaviours without first planning, preparing or indeed focusing on the needs of others involved.

Understanding and analysing others

Understanding other people and reading them right is vital for an effective outcome in most influencing situations. So the next stage in this process involves you in looking at other people. This means gathering as much information as possible about all the other people who are either involved or affected by your influencing issue. Some of the things you might like to think about are:

- the job they do
- what seems to turn them on and turn them off
- how they communicate with you and others
- talking/listening ratio
- body language used
- facial expressions used
- types of questions asked
- questions versus statements
- what skills, approaches and techniques do they use when influencing you
- what are your feelings about them.

> Think about your influencing issue. Firstly, list the people who were involved or affected by the issue. Try analysing them by using the questions above. How would this analysis have affected the way you influenced them?

Failure to do a thorough job at this stage in the process often leads to a less successful outcome for you or at worst total failure to influence!

> *When I started putting myself in the other person's shoes I found it was much easier to get them on board with me. It was just a matter of thinking it through beforehand.*
> **– Gordon Murray, engineering consultant**

Review

You should by this stage in the process have a greater understanding of the influencing environment, the others involved and yourself. Review and reflection is now appropriate before moving onto the next stage in the model.

> Assuming you are using the model to work through a real-life influencing issue, this is the stage at which you should make some notes about the key messages coming from your analysis of the environment, others involved and yourself. These notes will help you when you reach the final stage of the model – deciding on your influencing strategy.

Exploring skills and approaches

Having done your analysis you should now be in a position to think about the influencing approaches, skills and tactics to use. This may involve a variety of different approaches for different people in different situations, all of whom are being affected by your issue. For instance, you may have to influence:

○ your boss
○ your boss's boss
○ your work team
○ suppliers
○ groups of colleagues.

And indeed you may have to do this:

○ one-to-one
○ at a group meeting
○ as a formal presentation to a large audience
○ as an informal presentation at a meeting.

> ❝ *It seemed so easy when I talked it through with my boss. He was very encouraging and said he would support me if I could get my team and my colleagues on board as well. This was proving more difficult. Meetings often ended in a bit of a rabble, and I seemed to be getting nowhere. One-to-one it's easy – you're really only holding a conversation with a purpose – but I'll have to think more about how I influence all the others.* ❞
> **– Alex Barclay, human resources manager**

Think about the people you have to influence on a regular basis and categorise into two groups:

❑ Those you have some sort of authority over
❑ Those over whom you have no authority.

Often the position you find yourself in at this stage is one where you are "influencing without authority". This means that with many influencing situations you find yourself in you will have no formal authority or power over the person or people whom you are attempting to influence. This alone is challenging. In fact, in order to influence effectively you must take account of the other people's opinions, concerns and views on the issue. What works for one person or group may not work for others, and what works one-to-one may not work in a group meeting.

By this stage you will be well aware that the whole influencing process is not simply about stating a rational, assertive and well thought through case but involves significant time, energy and emotion on all fronts.

> Again using the same influencing issue, reflect upon the skills and approaches you used. How successful/unsuccessful were they? Why might this have been? Now taking account of the analysis you have done, what skills and approaches would you now use?

Deciding on your influencing strategy

> ❝ *This was the easy bit – having done my homework and lots of it, the strategy I had to follow became clear. It still wasn't going to be easy but before I used this model I would have fallen at the first hurdle and found it very difficult to pick myself up.* ❞
> **– Gordon Murray**

Having done a full analysis, deciding on your influencing strategy should now be much easier. The specific skills and approaches you use will vary from situation to situation and person to person. The important point here is to realise that you MUST use different ones for different people, environments and situations.

> Using the same issue yet again draw up your influencing strategy based on this model. Review how similar/different it is to the actual approach you used and reflect upon why this might be. What can you learn from this whole process?

> Now take a current influencing challenge that you are facing and apply the influencing model to it. Work through each of the stages and develop your influencing strategy.

Tips on seeing influencing as a process

One of the keys to successful influencing is accepting that it is part of a long-term process involving careful preparation and planning.

1. Influencing is a long-term process. It requires not only careful preparation and planning, but also the ability to establish and develop relationships with others and to deal with people both rationally and emotionally.
2. Reflecting about and reviewing the actual environment within which you are trying to influence helps you to understand the way things usually get done. This information is then useful for helping you to plan your influencing strategy.
3. In-depth self-awareness is vital: understanding how you come across to others, how they perceive you, what your typical influencing style is and, of course, your strengths and weaknesses.
4. Analyse the people you are attempting to influence. It is essential to put yourself into their shoes both when planning and during any influencing interaction. The important point is to appeal to them.
5. Using the right influencing style and adopting the correct approach for each of the parties concerned is fundamental to the success of your influencing interaction. So think it through and use different skills and approaches appropriately.
6. Follow the influencing model to ensure detailed analysis and preparation, and only then decide on your strategy.
7. Now for the hard bit – doing it!

What's in this chapter for you

Focus on the interaction
Influencing one-to-one
Influencing a group
Influential presentations
Influencing the boss

> ❝ *Successful influencing is all about getting people's commitment. Without that you haven't really influenced anyone – all you're doing is deluding yourself.* ❞
>
> **– Jim Wilson**

Think about it, how often do you feel that you have gained people's commitment? What makes you feel that way? What is it that encourages you to commit to someone else's ideas?

Focus on the interaction

The focus in this section will be on the actual face-to-face interactions you have with others. This includes influencing in one-to-one discussions, and influencing a group, part of a group or a large audience. Dialogue will already be taking place during your planning and preparation phase (which as we have already seen can be very time consuming). The dialogue during that phase, while using many of the same skills, will be predominantly to:

○ network
○ research and test your ideas
○ test others' views
○ establish your credibility
○ plant ideas for nurturing later on.

So in real terms influencing is actually going on all the time as you are constantly sowing seeds into people's minds. However, in order to get a decision, to gain commitment or to get buy-in (at any stage in the process) you probably have to have a meeting or possibly do a presentation to deal with these formalities.

Whatever the stage in the process, the purpose of any interaction is to get evidence of long-term commitment rather than quick wins. For instance look for:

○ suggestions that build or extend your ideas
○ offers to join you to work on the issue
○ conscious and direct support for your ideas
○ exploratory and inquisitive questions.

The more formal influencing situations demand you to draw on your full range of skills, knowledge and behaviours. Whatever form the influencing interaction takes there are three distinct stages you should always complete:

○ planning and preparing
○ dialogue
○ review.

The tips that follow concentrate on the more formal and organised aspects of an influencing dialogue.

Influencing one-to-one

This is probably the most common type of influencing situation and one that you probably find the least frightening. In fact many of the one-to-one discussions you have each day probably involve you influencing the other person about something, e.g.:

○ getting a member of your team to do a job for you
○ persuading a colleague to use the services your team provide
○ persuading your partner about a holiday destination
○ influencing your son or daughter to do their homework
○ appraising a member of your team
○ dealing with a poor performer.

Think of two or three recent one-to-one discussions that have involved some aspect of influencing. What was the purpose and outcome of the discussion? Review what went well and why, and what went badly and why. In the discussions where you were successful in influencing, what skills, techniques and approaches did you use? Were they the same in each case? If not, why not?

Some of the comments I hear during training sessions about one-to-one influencing would indicate that people find one-to-one discussions the least challenging of all the influencing situations they find themselves in.

“ *If I know the person, influencing one-to-one isn't a problem.* ”

“ *One-to-one is easy as long as you listen, question and adapt your style to meet their needs as well.* ”

“ *I don't worry about one-to-one influencing. After all it's only a conversation between two people.* ”

“ *Influencing one-to-one is easy, especially if you know the person and can prepare accordingly by thinking through beforehand what turns them on and off.* ”
– Participants on influencing skills training sessions

Even if you don't know the person, following some fairly simple guidelines will give you a real advantage:

❑ **Preparation**
■ What is your objective and purpose? Write it down
■ Think about the other person, their style, what turns them on/off, their power bases, their views about the topic
■ Get all the information together, focus on facts and feelings
■ What are your power bases?
■ What style, approach and tactics will you use
❑ **Discussion**
■ State your view of the issue – the problem, the cause, the possibilities

- Gain an understanding of their perceptions about the issue – question, listen, reflect and summarise
- Get commitment to work together – explore information, use examples, give feedback
- Explore possible solutions – share ideas, build on ideas, visualise outcomes
- Share reactions – listen, question, test understanding, explore alternatives, jointly work to a solution
- Summarise and agree outcomes – clarify, summarise, plan for action
- ❑ **Review and reflect**
- Did you meet your objective?
- What approaches/skills etc. worked/didn't work?
- What have you learned about the other person for next time?
- What have you learned for the future?

❝ Having a plan when I meet someone one-to-one really helps me, especially when I don't know the person very well – it really helps to keep me on track. When it's really important I sometimes rehearse the discussion first with a friend. ❞
– Sylvia Brown

Influencing a group

Most of you who work in a business environment attend meetings, probably on a boringly regular basis! In the context of influencing there are two important yet subtly different types of meeting situation.

- ○ Influencing from within the meeting group. This is when you are one of several people discussing a topic where everyone will have their own perceptions and views of the issue. Usually the goal is for the group to reach an acceptable outcome for all involved.
- ○ Influencing to a group. This usually means that you are the instigator of the meeting. You have called the people together in order to put forward your case and influence them to buy into your ideas on an issue or problem.

Think about influencing meetings that you have attended recently. Reflect on the purpose of the meeting and use a table like that shown below to review and learn:

Meeting purpose	Type of meeting 1 or 2	My level of involvement	Desired outcome reached	Why/why not?

❝ I find managing meetings the most difficult of all. Everyone wants to have their say and often people are more emotional than I thought they'd be, especially when they see they have allies in the group. ❞
– Gordon Murray

For each of the two group influencing situations there are key points to remember and in each case having a process to follow during the meeting can be helpful.

Key points to remember when influencing within a group are:

❏ Remember that everyone who is involved will be both influencer and influenced!
❏ Influencing within a group almost always involves compromise so you should be willing to be flexible and adaptable.
❏ State your views clearly and simply.
❏ Listen to others views.
❏ Question the others to ensure understanding and for clarification.
❏ Summarise regularly – again for understanding and clarity.
❏ Observe others' behaviour. Look for clues and cues in their non-verbal behaviour as well as what they say.
❏ Face any conflict or confrontation by remaining calm and encouraging the individual to explore the issue concerned. Often giving people a chance to speak and be listened to will take the heat out of the situation.

"Nothing gives one person so much advantage over another as to remain cool and unruffled under all circumstances!"
– Thomas Jefferson

Key points to remember when influencing to a group.

- ❑ What style, approach and tactics will you use?
- ❑ Are you trying to "tell or sell" your ideas.
- ❑ Lobby people before the meeting to test your ideas.
- ❑ Identify those people who will support you and those who will challenge you.
- ❑ Anticipate counter proposals and arguments and prepare how you will deal with them
- ❑ Identify the key decision makers. They are not always the most obvious people.
- ❑ Identify the other key influencers. Gaining their support can be highly beneficial to your case.

Researchers have shown on many occasions that meetings can be far more productive and meaningful if a process is established and followed.

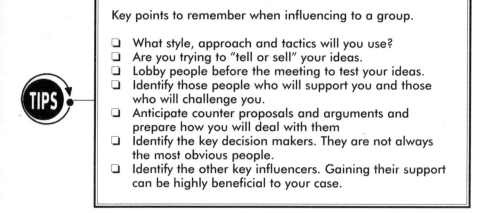

Think back to the meetings you made notes about earlier. Did any of these meetings follow a process? What did it involve? Did it work? How did you feel about the process? Can you learn from it?

❝ *When I'm in meetings often all I want is to have my say, be listened to and understood. I know I can't always get my own way, but sometimes I feel that my ideas are worth while and could add value to the eventual outcome.* ❞
– Participant on Ashridge's Influencing Strategies and Skills programme

One process which many of my programme participants have found to be a useful addition to their toolkit is:

- ❑ Agree with all group members what the objective of the meeting is.

- ❑ Agree a finish time.
- ❑ Allocate or agree roles:
  - ■ coordinator (or chairperson)
  - ■ note or minute taker
  - ■ timekeeper
- ❑ Restate the objective and write it up on a flipchart for all to see and be reminded of.
- ❑ Collect everyone's views about the issue:
  - ■ allocate a short period of time to hear everyone's views (the time allocated will depend on the time available for the meeting and the number of participants) – usually no longer than five minutes per person (be ruthless about the five minutes – fairness is vital here)
  - ■ ask each person to note on a flipchart their key points at the end of their time
  - ■ make sure you have the same time to put your views across
- ❑ Examine the notes on the flipchart and summarise the views and situation.
- ❑ Open the meeting up for discussion – questioning, testing understanding and summarising – always ensuring that people are listened to.
- ❑ Work towards an outcome which should be agreed by all. Look for common ground, build on mutual interests and be willing to compromise.
- ❑ Look for a win–win outcome by incorporation of ideas from others.
- ❑ Agree the outcome and plan the way ahead. Write it down and restate it just to be sure.

Having a process like the one above or developing a similar process that fits with your particular environment and personality has several benefits.

- ○ There will be clarity right from the beginning regarding the objective and each person's role.
- ○ Often simply having the opportunity to have their opinion heard is all a person wants.
- ○ By sharing views early on you get a clear idea of where each person stands and how much disagreement exists. Often it's less than you think and even then it's sometimes only little things that people aren't overly concerned about.
- ○ This sort of open discussion helps to build trust, respect and ultimately your credibility.

How do you feel when at a meeting someone asks for your opinion and everyone actually listens to you? Then perhaps someone follows up with a question encouraging you to expand further or someone builds on your idea!

Influential presentations

Most presentations regardless of audience size involve influencing. Whatever the topic or purpose you will be influencing the audience in some way, shape or form even if it is only to give you a hearing!

Many people find giving a presentation quite daunting and many always will, but assuming that you accept that preparation and planning are vital for success I can assure you that even the most polished and confident speaker will have invested time and energy to do this.

Think of the last really influential presentation that you attended. What made you listen? Why was it influential? What did the speaker do to make it interesting?

The following key points should help you to focus on the important issues for making your presentation influential.
- ❏ Focus on your audience. Who are they? What will they know? How will you get them to listen?
- ❏ Gain their attention. Give your audience a selfish reason to listen.
- ❏ Show your enthusiasm. If you are not committed and enthusiastic about the issue don't give a presentation!
- ❏ During the presentation use analogies, stories and metaphors. These help to bring the talk to life and make it interesting
- ❏ State your objective, purpose or goal early on.
- ❏ State the facts, clearly and logically and give examples. Show them you know your stuff.

❏ Start with a bang. First impressions are very important. Make it interesting, challenging, controversial or whatever it takes to get them interested and listening. Rehearse it and memorise it.

❏ Develop a memorable closing statement linked to your opening. Remind them of your key points, ask for action and restate your objective. Remember that if they haven't listened throughout your talk all the gimmicks in the world won't catch them now!

❏ Any visual aids should be simple, clear and add value for your audience.

❏ Remember to focus on how you are using your voice and what you look like (your body language) as well as the words.

❏ Review your presentations immediately. Make a note of what went well, what went badly, and what you would do differently next time.

Do you want to know more about presentations? Have a look at *Persuasive Presentations* by Michael James

Watch other people, especially "professional" influencers – politicians, sales people, trainers, etc. What techniques do they use to make their presentations more influential?

Get a trusted friend or colleague to give you feedback on your influencing presentations. Initially, ask them to focus on particular parts of the talk or else on particular skills then build up to getting feedback on the whole talk. Getting the right person here is important in order to get balanced feedback – both positive and developmental stuff.

❝ *Giving a presentation for any purpose makes me nervous but I know that nerves are an important part of the process and as long as I have done my preparation and know my stuff the nerves soon disappear once I start talking.* ❞
– Jim Wilson

Influencing the boss

Do you ever find yourself saying "I just don't understand why she keeps interfering." "I'm fed up; he's always poking his nose in – he's a real pain." Perhaps your relationship with your boss isn't all it should be!

Remember that apart from your staff your boss is probably the other person you most frequently have to influence. Sometimes this is on quite simple issues such as getting some time off, or meeting to agree the holiday rota, but it can also be on many more challenging issues like your annual appraisal or getting their support for a new project.

Research has shown that effective managers take time and put significant effort into managing their relationship with their boss. They are often the people who can help you the most to get things done and very often they are likely to be a key influencer about your next promotion or pay rise.

> **❝** *It took me a while to realise it, but my relationship with my boss is really important. When I get his support and commitment he really is the biggest ally I have. He helps me to get access to the right people, to get resources and often acts as devil's advocate to help me see all sides of an issue.* **❞**
> **– Richard Williams**

How would you describe your relationship with your boss? Write down some key words explaining it

So what can you do to help in the process of influencing your boss? Here are some ideas.

❑ Spend time getting to know your boss. What are their strengths and weaknesses, management style, work priorities and goals? You have got to know whom you are dealing with. Time spent doing this will pay dividends in the end.

- ❑ Plan and prepare well, and work out your strategy. Bosses are busy people. Don't waste their time. Use it well and they'll listen again.
- ❑ Watch them in action, how they act at meetings, doing presentations, with their boss.
- ❑ Put yourself in their shoes. Think about the limitations on their situation. Remember that your boss has a boss too!
- ❑ Don't surprise your boss. Your boss has to trust you so prepare them well especially if you are influencing during a meeting where others will be present.
- ❑ Show loyalty to your boss. Support them when they need it. Reciprocity is important for developing a trusting and respectful relationship.
- ❑ If you disagree with your boss, say so, but back up your view with clear analysis and reasoning.
- ❑ Note also the tips given earlier in the section on one-to-one discussions.

It may be worth putting in a short health warning here. Don't depend too much on one senior person. Bosses move on, get promoted and sometimes they even let you down! It is always worth developing relationships with several more senior people. Research has shown that one of the major causes of an individual derailing in their career is loss of a key sponsor or supporter.

Influencing others is largely about relationship development, self-awareness and awareness of others. Gaining commitment, support and buy-in from others is crucial for successful influencing.

A final thought

Influencing others
Needs patience and
Flexibility
Listen actively to
Understand others' views.
Express your views fluently
Not aggressively
Check understanding and above all
Enthusiasm is key to success.

Other books about influencing

Bragg, M. (1996) *Reinventing Influence*. Pitman Publishing.
Bryce, L. (1991) *The Influential Manager*. BCA.
Gillen, T. (1995) *Positive Influencing Skills*. Institute of Personnel and
    Development.
Huczynski, A. (1996) *Influencing within Organisations*. Prentice Hall.
James, M. (1997) *Persuasive Presentations*. David Grant Publishing.
Lambert, T. (1996) *The Power of Influence*. Nicholas Brealey Publish-
    ing.